M000313679

The Voyage

The
Voyage

Christopher Manners

Poetica Press

First published in the USA
by Poetica Press 2019
an imprint of Sophia Perennis
© Christopher Manners 2018

For information, address:
Poetica Press, Ltd.
PO Box 253 El Prado, NM 87529
info@sophiaperennis.com

Paperback: 978-1-59731-181-6

Cover design: Michael Schrauzer

To my parents with love

CONTENTS

On a Walk

Walking in my deeply pensive way,
I notice this weary man nearby,
seeing the lonely sorrow in his eyes,
the heaviness which he does convey,
while his pain seems only to rise
and encompass the perplexing sky,
sensitive to that common dismay,
that innate suffering which does lie
at existence's core, always the prey
of unfulfilled hopes as we decry
our so swift and ruthless decay,
always aware that we soon shall die.

And yet there is boundless beauty here,
amid the majestic mountains and trees,
as I hear these singing birds sublime,
reminded of a wondrous female face,
and the vastness of the mighty seas,
the stars of the endless cosmos clear,
which even as we're ravaged by time,
we can explore as we valiantly steer
towards greater harmonies to align,
striving to those distant shores to trace,
as we have the capacity to truly revere
the glory of beauty and of art divine,
the ability to voyage forth and create,
as that radiance does fleetingly shine,
that soaring splendor to always extol,
providing solace in our struggling state,
serving, even briefly, to uplift and console
for all the agonies of this barren land,
while we endure the arduous hole,
always yearning for that freedom grand.

The Mariner

An old mariner long did wander
for what seemed many a grueling life,
through the ocean as he did ponder
the significance of his ceaseless strife,
through each ruthless, rising wave,
while in his distress he could never find
any precious land, peacefully secure,
always fated through the years to brave
the endless battle in his beleaguered mind,
worse than the tempests he did flee,
which repeatedly he did wearily endure,
while he yearned so deeply to see,
to unite with a grand and majestic port,
yet all the mist continued to obscure
his lacking sight, while his inner fort
was collapsing in that darkness deep,
growing swiftly, as he could only court
more plaguing emptiness and disdain,
struggling through fierce winds to keep
his strength, while all the fog did distort
his solitary path through the dire pain,
left in that bewilderment to weep.

Yet after one particular storm extreme,
he began to search and contemplate,
beyond all the chaos which did teem,
venturing deeper as he did explore,
and in his persistent, focused state,
he uncovered this radiance in his core,
this wonder which was waiting to beam,
more luminous than the most brilliant star,
which he sensed was always there,

as that old fog no longer did bar,
and the endless potentialities did flow,
while he soared past all his despair,
entirely transformed with his new glow,
free of the abyss he long did bear,
and after all that struggle and dismay,
he now would wander no more,
with boundless joy as he made his way
finally ahead to the illumined shore,
as the glorious harbour was beyond all
his limited thoughts of the past,
returning, as he heard the call,
to his serene home, always to last.

The King

Travelling many days through the heat,
a sorrowful man, completely distraught,
finally a venerable sage did greet,
as his assistance he eagerly sought.
"I'm not satisfied with this life I lead:
I've reached certain goals as I did aspire,
but then they only planted the seed
for greater desires and misery's fire,
as this emptiness always does impede.
Bewildered, I'm not able to find
that revered peace for which I yearn,
that calmness for my stormy mind,
while in this restlessness I burn."

Turning his attention from the vast sky,
now the old sage did gracefully reply.
"There was a certain King of yore,
who also felt this similar immense pain,
deeply anguished in his very core,
as his existence he began to disdain.
So in his way he promptly then did decide
his cherished kingdom to proudly expand,
sending his formidable cavalry to ride,
battling his rivals for more precious land,
and his powerful realm did quickly grow,
as more lofty castles he then did raise,
as his treasury did impressively flow,
while his populace did duly praise.
So he built additional structures grand
to continue glorifying his flourishing reign,
and majestic towers to strikingly stand,
with wide renown throughout the plain,

often exalted by his triumphal band,
with increasing influence to boldly attain.
Then an even larger army he did mount,
each veteran knight ready with their lance,
with his ambitions as an endless fount,
as he longed even farther to advance
into remote territories to hungrily explore,
consumed by such a covetous trance,
with rising aspirations always to adore,
and strategizing with every chance
to extend further, pressing even more.

Yet still dissatisfied the King did feel,
flooded by this insatiable ache,
which left him in distress as he did reel,
as furiously he then did break
a valued artifact which he did obtain
in a land so distant from home,
as he was beset by sorrow's stain,
always weary as he did roam.
And this King continually would extend
his palace at home while he always did stir,
yet all his pain he never could mend,
never aware of his inner palace pure."

That Blissful Time

Bring me back to that blissful time
when I just played the length of the day,
amidst the glory of those fields green,
when the cherished birds would chime,
always jubilant in that buoyant way
under the illuminating Sun serene,
before all this weary distress and pain
and all the aching tedium now near,
back to the splendor of that plain,
in those golden days to revere,
with never any sorrowful weight,
nor any aching burdens to hold,
when I soared in that ecstatic state,
that underlying wonder to behold.
As I was immersed in that play dear,
forgetting myself, past that insatiable fire,
I was so vibrant and triumphantly free,
the world unveiled and suddenly clear,
beyond the woeful bondage of desire
and into that unity which did enthrall,
basking then in that beaming glee,
winged with the birds as they did call,
as in that grand joy I was able to see
the deep and connected essence of all.

Emptiness

How can I endure these days
of endless emptiness to despise,
in this ravaging nothingness caught,
in this deep and devastating haze?
With absolutely nothing to prize,
and nothing meaningful to be sought,
these invasions continue to raze
my last remnants of dwindling hope,
always with this cruel war to be fought,
increasingly agonizing now to cope.

And what is there really to gain
by enduring this tyrannous torment,
by persisting on this miserable plain,
while all this anguish doesn't relent?
Why struggle? Why even survive,
amidst this ruthlessly constant pain?
What is there truly to derive,
while the sorrow does always drain?
Immersed in this ocean of despair,
with scarcely a drop of joy brief,
I find now that I no longer care,
resentful of this punishing stay
in these waves of endless grief,
while the storm clouds never stray,
where I'm never granted relief,
yelling furiously at the sky grey,
while my loneliness continues to leave
me in these ruins of desolate dismay,

solitary in this vast cosmos to weave
my laments through the restless day.
Only the Void does understand,
my only lasting companion here,
while truly connecting in this land,
with the mind's complexities immense,
is essentially impossible as I fear,
with such disparities in thoughts intense,
in myriad emotions and aspirations dear,
while only the Void is my enduring home,
always in these tedious depths to steer,
continuously in my weariness to roam
these empty spaces and caverns near,
as for so many years I've known
this abysmal lack through every tear,
which has swiftly expanded and grown,
this pervading emptiness my only peer
while so many dreams have quickly flown.

Trapped on this barren ground,
and never able as the birds to soar,
my ceaseless questions always resound,
while I'm battered in my very core.
Yet who can I question in this storm?
Who can I turn to now in my distress?
God doesn't seem of the personal form,
as I'm left with no one to address;
and God as the remote Absolute
bewilders in that inscrutable way,
seeming always perpetually mute,
that infinite energy remaining unknown,

with the harsh universe silent each day,
in this dire nothingness and anguish,
plagued by the boundless Void's maze,
while I'm struggling so painfully alone,
only in emptiness as l languish,
sinking in this wretched haze.

The Prison

I awoke in perplexity years prior
and found myself strangely here,
trapped in this dark prison dire,
with an explanation never near,
filled with agony's endless fire,
and flooded by many a tear.
Alone in this despairing state,
my captor I've never seen,
bewildered by my unjust fate,
as I long for those fields green,
blocked by these bars of weight,
while for so long I've been keen
to make that escape and flee,
yet success I've never found,
as the serene sky I've yet to see,
while my aching laments resound.

I must revolt with all my will
against the vexing tyrant cruel
who imprisoned me in this way,
who leaves me in this misery still,
so ravaging in his remote rule,
who created this suffering dismay,
all this desolate pain without rest,
which I can never understand,
long exiled from my true land,
with these weary days to detest.
With my driving tenacity deep,
to all my inner energies I turn,
no longer willing to always weep,
as for sweet freedom I so yearn,

deliverance which I must find,
no longer in this torture to wane,
with my strong resolve of mind,
for cherished liberty to gain.

To the Sage: A Vision

Engulfed in recurring torment
and weary of the constant cage,
the wretched war never did relent,
forced each afflicted day to wage,
and so to a wise elder I finally went,
who was the oldest in the town,
confiding in him with my lament,
while in the vile flood I did drown.
"So many ambitions I did achieve,
so many majestic summits I did attain,
yet strangely I still painfully grieve,
still in this emptiness which does chain,
always with this deep chasm to bear,
with this restless anguish to deplore,
as these attackers always tear,
while I yearn for a peaceful shore."

"You must visit this certain sage,
who lives on a distant island alone,
preserving the wisdom of a prior age,
who has ventured into the unknown,
as his radiance did always glow,
who can assist you in your plight,
one of the few now who deeply know,
as you must voyage with your might.
But in order your seriousness to convey,
a certain offering you must provide:
the last column which still does stand
of his old temple, which in its glorious day
once inspired so many bravely to ride
above the tired struggles of this land,
though sadly in ruins now to bewail,

destroyed by those blind invaders cruel,
as upon the plain they did descend,
forcing the sage's exile as he did sail,
missing for so many years my old friend,
fleeing to the seas for his renewal.
And with that column you can commence
a new soaring temple together to mold,
to tower on that island, so immense,
as you will rise with your efforts bold;
only the Infinite your anguish will still,
the boundless Source which pervades all,
and only the Infinite shall truly fulfill,
as you respond to that perennial call,
and so this trek you must now take,
vigilantly on your crucial course to tend,
with other desires to finally forsake,
towards this sage as you strive to ascend."

So I proceeded without delay,
venturing into the dark forest ahead
towards that old temple on my way,
with rejuvenated energy as I did tread.
Yet moving into perilous, foreign ground,
I was ambushed swiftly by two on horse,
stealing my provisions as they did astound,
and striking me with their vicious force,
defending vigorously with many a yell
but overpowered as I attempted to shield,
left bloodied and wounded where I fell,
as they sped off finally into the field.
I lay there through the aching night,
enduring all the agony of that pain,

yet I was still constant in my resolve,
and in the morning I resumed my flight,
as my fears did quickly dissolve,
still searching for that sacred plain.

Soon the temple in its ruins I found,
nobly situated on that hill as I saw,
sensing a certain wonder profound
as I approached with my reverent awe.
And the one standing column was there,
still triumphantly tall amid the rest,
a beacon of lasting hope over despair,
as I was inspired to continue my quest.
Yet the column was a burden to carry forth,
as I struggled towards the nearby port,
slowly walking on my path north,
testing the strength of my interior fort,
eventually reaching the harbour grand
and attaining a vessel to traverse,
with the turbulent sea then to withstand,
while my wounds I still did nurse.

Starting my journey through each wave,
I was alone to contend with the harsh skies,
battling my recurring doubts as I did brave
the rough and ruthless waters obscure,
while solely that sage I continued to prize,
always reminding myself to endure.
Soon a rapid pirate vessel fierce
emerged with menace and opened fire,
attempting my humble ship to pierce,
as I contemplated then my death dire,
struggling those merciless pirates to flee,
with their formidable shots alarmingly near,

causing my increasing panic and grief,
frantically bearing the torture of a spear,
yet in the heavy fog they couldn't see,
gratefully losing me as I did veer,
continuing my course with such relief,
towards that revered sage to steer.

Finally his remote home I did find,
an island of calm amidst each storm,
with such elation in my jubilant mind,
as I anticipated his welcome warm,
and I knew then that I would never perish,
as his island was illuminated by the beam
of the perpetual sun to always cherish,
embracing the joy which always does teem.

The Wondrous Lady

I was walking in deep despair,
in my anguish which does torment,
with that restless ennui to bear,
and despondent in that descent,
when a wondrous lady I did find,
with her striking smile as I did glance,
freed from that desolation blind,
as I was lifted from my barren trance,
as her celestial face did remind
of the endless glory of Eternity High,
filled in my core with peace serene,
and inspired so suddenly to fly,
with that stunning radiance in her eyes,
towering over the vibrant fields green,
watching gallant chariots in the skies,
as all the cosmos did then convene,
jubilantly unbound as I did rise
to the majesty of the greater plane,
open to marvels never before seen
and triumphant over misery's pain.
Rejuvenated by her boundless shine,
I knew the Infinite that blessèd day,
with that blissful unity to commence,
embraced by the love of the Divine,
no longer in that weary abyss of grey,
immersed in the one ocean immense,
awakening towards the sacred way,
my soul ascending in its noble flight,
on that voyage to purely sense,
towards the consciousness of Light.
And yet never will she know me,

vanishing so swiftly as she did leave,
as a fleeting bird which soared by,
as never again will I ever see
those eyes which illumined the sky,
left alone now as I grieve.

The Seeker

After travelling for several long days,
he finally reached the revered hermit old,
the seeking knight in an anguished haze,
while his urgent request he now did mold.
"Dear hermit, I come to you in great need,
after hearing of your unveiling vision clear,
as I yearn for understanding complete,
as this deep longing now does exceed
all other aspirations which were once dear,
grateful now to have this cherished seat
amidst your serenity, in your sacred home,
as the sweetest of knowledge I must attain,
no longer content merely to roam,
towards limited pleasures on this plain,
feeling more caged under the sky's dome
and so eager that illumination to gain."

"To have this great yearning intense
already shows much progress to commend,
but before you are ready to commence
on the path towards knowledge to ascend,
there is more that you must now fulfill,
with more arduous struggle to contend,
and more crucial labour awaiting still,
while your resolve must never bend.
First you must defeat that creature cruel,
who this poor land continues to ravage,
who torments with his voracious rule,
always attacking with that rage savage,
who all the farmers and villagers disdain,
so insatiable with his hunger fierce,
as you too have suffered personal pain

from this creature continuing to pierce,
which you have known your life entire,
as the tyranny of his agonizing force
has left you in an empty desert dire,
but it is finally time to take the course
and conquer with courage higher.
Yet it will take devoted strength,
as this ruthless creature does deceive,
as you must prepare for a fight of length,
as many in their efforts have been short,
unable to master as they flee and grieve,
turning back to the safety of the fort
of their mundane lives and vain routine,
no longer willing to sacrifice and endure,
content only with what they have seen,
while neglecting that sight most pure.

But this creature you must vanquish
in a particular way, or he just will keep
returning and always coming back,
while you only weaken and languish,
with that sorrow which pervades deep,
forced to face each relentless attack,
striving on, but still sensing that lack.
So you must now travel and proceed
to the greatest craftsman in this land,
who will shape for you the proper sword
in his mighty forge, generous and grand,
and with critical instruction he will lead
you on your way, valiantly toward
that vicious creature as you will stand
capable of victory, for peace restored.

After you overcome the creature vile,
then you can return swiftly to me,
and I will guide you in my style,
assisting you to joyously grow,
to be free of all bondage and weight,
as you aspire so boldly to see,
to cross the kingdom's river great,
where washing waters always flow,
to reach the bliss of that state,
and finally in your core to know."

So the knight went off on his path,
deeply appreciative of the hermit wise,
eager to tame that creature's wrath,
and continuing now with resolute eyes
onward to the craftsman's forge
which so ardently he did prize,
through the valley and every gorge,
envisioning that creature's demise.

Now he suddenly caught the glance
of a radiant lady's striking smile,
as she approached him with delight,
her splendor leaving him in a trance,
as they conversed then for a while
the knight yearning with so much might
to stay with this maiden to adore,
quickly engulfed by an internal fight,
held by this chain in his very core,
while her eyes carried him to a height
which he had never sensed before,
longing to embrace, as now the night
crept over the kingdom and its shore.

While her wonder did so enthrall
the captivated knight, in his distress,
he knew the pull of the greater call,
and finally did solemnly address.

"Despite all your glory to exalt,
I've decided strongly that I must leave,
our connection important to halt,
as I must resist and resume my trek,
my steady route keen to retrieve,
with our grief now vital to check."

And with streaming tears on his cheek,
the knight his mission did maintain,
carrying on the next day as he did seek
his goal with new zeal, as he did sustain
his solitary passage to the required peak,
struggling ahead and not willing to wane.

Now an energetic man did strangely appear,
rushing forward with soaring elation,
yelling to the knight as he came near,
his frenzy heard through the entire nation.
"Gold! We've discovered gold!
Come quickly as vast riches await,
with boundless wealth now to behold,
and endless possibilities to create!"

As this jubilant voice he heard,
he zealously felt the drive to acquire
his precious share, that enticing glow,
as by this opportunity he was stirred,
grappling now with a furious fire,
and immersed in his burning woe.

And yet as much as he did savor,
with much tenacity he steadied his mind,
firmly dedicated as he wouldn't waver,
as greater purpose he continued to find.

"Leave me now. Leave me alone.
Such an acquisition would only feed
more unquenchable desire to bewail,
as all your gold I really don't need,
as only the pristine waters I must sail,
as from my infancy I have now grown."

So he continued on his way,
travelling through the vibrant field,
while the winds increasingly did sway,
hoping still that decisive sword to wield.
And now in the distance he curiously saw
a growing crowd quickly gathering around
this singer charming with his song,
while his voice did remarkably resound,
leaving the listeners in absorbed awe,
while he continued his performance long,
and he felt this new hunger as he did view
the attached multitude as they did praise,
with all that eminent adoration to accrue,
the knight immersed again in a haze.

Yet marshaling all of his critical power,
this too he eventually passed by,
waging another battle at that hour
until he was able again to sense
the perpetual serenity of the sky,
amidst all its vastness immense,
as his concentrated mind did tower

over all his prior thoughts tense,
now focusing all his strength to reach
the honourable craftsman, his aim,
his inner castle never to breach,
as he extinguished every flame.

In the evening he continued to tire
until finally he saw the forge ahead,
that impressive structure to admire,
as he was filled with rising relief,
and towards the door he did tread,
ready to be free of all his grief.

He was welcomed with a smile,
led graciously and deeper inside,
observing each piece, many a pile,
as the craftsman now did gladly guide
him to his sword, already complete,
already in anticipation to provide,
and it was truly stunning to meet,
emboldening with its majestic design,
his crucial fate inspiring to greet,
with his sword and its wondrous shine.

In the Storm

It is immensely difficult to be free
of the painful wheel, as again I return
to sail once more in this raging sea,
where all this agony continues to churn,
where every island which I boldly pursue,
which initially seems so fruitful and grand,
is always barren and lacking in its way,
never fulfilled in such desolate land,
while all these ambitions I can't subdue,
so restless under their voracious sway,
endless aspirations which only result
in more deep disappointment and pain,
weary of the vicious waves which ensue,
which leave me so battered each day,
these flooding sorrows unable to halt,
while this grueling journey I must disdain,
trapped in this ruthless storm's assault,
as existence only continues to drain.

The Builder

I was walking slowly on my way
through remote forests alone,
in my dissatisfaction and dismay,
as life's significance had flown,
and this old man I then found,
building this structure on his own,
toiling with that regular sound,
in his weariness as he did groan,
with his massive task profound,
slowly carrying each heavy stone.

"Old man, what are you doing here,
labouring now in this grueling heat,
surely with aching exhaustion near,
as this building you strive to complete?"

"No, sadly it will never be complete.
When I was a young man around
your present age, with agony great
I was always excruciatingly bound,
and so I ventured out then to meet
a certain seer, aware of Divine fate,
who I bombarded with questions tense,
inquiring into our suffering state,
and all my excessive pain immense,
as the human experience I did berate.
So the seer then did explain
the path for suffering to transcend,
the way with the Godhead to unite,
to be free of this struggling plane,
yet this process to finally ascend
and reach that most blissful Light

I recognized to be of difficulty extreme,
an anguished and arduous process long,
possibly requiring many lives to stream,
and still too much agony to endure,
needing so much fortitude strong,
while all our ceaseless aspirations stir.
Tired of this universe's vile stage
and with revolt as my escalating desire,
then in my boiling and mounting rage,
swiftly I set numerous trees on fire,
disdaining creation and all its pain
with surging wrath impossible to tame,
gazing out at the smoldering plain,
burning down a massive forest entire,
with many animals dying in that flame,
as I watched all that destruction dire.

And then this higher spirit came down
with my harsh punishment to declare,
as I realized that I soon would drown
in this torment of cruel despair.
So I was condemned for endless years
to constant labour on this sorrowful soil,
draining me with all my tortured tears,
and always trapped in this wretched toil,
always in this vicious solitude to work
under these oppressive, merciless skies,
while my loneliness continues to lurk,
as this existence I can only despise."

The Cruelty of Life

This poor, miserable man I knew
searched through most of his life,
but love he was never able to find,
while his aching loneliness only grew,
constantly battling that gloomy strife,
his eyes revealing his suffering mind.
So many various ladies of lives diverse
over the arduous years he did meet,
through so many dinners to converse,
yet a connection would never ensue,
as he would walk back with weary feet
to his empty home in despair to stew.
Finally then at the age of fifty-five,
he found a wondrous lady to adore,
as together they did joyously thrive,
starting to heal his battered core.
Their deep love, a profound well,
they mutually did pronounce,
yet one week later she then fell,
overcome by her dire disease,
which so rapidly then did pounce,
as her life so swiftly did cease.
Considering all this agony rife,
this is the cruelty of life.

The Founding of Croton

Assailed by illness and weak,
Myscellus now questioned the Divine,
as for deep understanding he did seek,
so bewildered by the world's design,
and all the suffering he now did face,
as he longed so deeply to be free
of all his pain, of the useless race,
yearning finally to behold and see.

Soon Apollo in his glory came down
to speak with this man in dismay,
visiting the Greek in his humble town,
stunning him on this momentous day.
"You must travel west now and found
a crucial colony on wondrous Italian land,
the new city meant in its way to resound,
to flourish in wisdom and then expand."

"But why? Why do you call on me?
I must now with reverence ask,
as I worry of that dangerous sea,
so perplexed by this appointed task."

"For reality to really uncover and know,
your mission you must now complete,
labouring for that limitless bliss to meet,
as the endless ocean does flow."

"Yet I am too weary and unwell
for this mission now to undertake,
as my agony continues to swell,
while my body continues to ache.
How can I so suddenly leave

my precious home, everything here,
this land which I treasure so dear,
surely a further cause to grieve?"

"If you seek that knowledge supreme,
then you must certainly abandon all,
in pursuit of that boundless beam,
no longer through desires to fall,
and when at your destination you arrive,
you will be free of all sorrow to endure,
as you must now proceed and strive,
voyaging to that joy most pure."

So after radiant Apollo did confide,
inspired Myscellus many colonists did enlist,
heading to the nearest port, as he did decide
to embark on this critical expedition ahead,
commencing his route in the sea's mist,
even as the unknown he now did dread.

With his growing gratitude immense,
his rising hopes quickly grew,
and he began now even to sense
much deep devotion among his crew,
as his leadership they did adore,
focused in their bold efforts of might,
as a majestic eagle aspiring to soar,
endeavouring to reach that new height.

Yet a distressing storm, viciously fierce,
soon bombarded them on their path,
now threatening their vessel to pierce,
and unleashing such relentless wrath,

as the engulfing tempest did pound
their humble ship, as they did pray,
turning to the sky with each anxious shout,
through the winds of menacing sound,
struggling to bear the ravaging day,
their minds filled with panic and doubt,
as Myscellus questioned the entire quest,
its meaning amid such disarray,
as his strength it did repeatedly test,
unsure if they could continue their way.

So through each ruthless wave,
through that turbulent chaos to steer,
he now battled his darkening despair,
with his worsening illness still to brave,
with the crew only showing more fear,
sensing the anguish pervading the air.
And as they were tossed with furious force,
he longed for land, safe and serene,
with the vessel wavering on its course,
as he recalled now the vibrant green
of the fields of his childhood home,
where in such delight he once did roam.

Finally he saw the cherished shore,
approaching now with renewed strength,
with a sense of jubilation in his core
after traversing that arduous length,
the crew disembarking to explore,
searching for the location ideal
for their new settlement to adore,
and preparing to build with zeal.
On the shore Myscellus soon did meet
an elder man, of tranquil mind,
who came forward with purpose to greet,

who seemed content the Greek to find.
"I am a sage and hermit old,
with the foresight that you would be here,
now ready for your colony to mold,
after the purifying waters you did sail,
grateful to see you, to be near,
aware of your suffering and its scale,
as I must now direct and teach,
with sacred knowledge to soon reach."

"But why is it my mission to start
this colony here on foreign soil?
I yearn for peace in my heart,
only exhausted by life's aching toil."

"Soon in the city which you shall raise,
a prodigious philosopher shall reside,
a successor of the grand line of sight,
who shall quickly inspire and amaze
not merely with his ideas to stride,
but with his depth, his inner light.
He shall be Pythagoras by name,
meant with the underlying Source to unite,
and the mysteries of the cosmos to tame,
as he will bring others to that height,
with understanding of the soul to provide,
compassionate to our struggle on this plain,
with his dedicated followers to guide,
to expound on the One which does reign.
So it is vital to found this city to cherish,
to be a centre of triumphant wisdom high,
recurring wisdom which in all ages does fly,
as the immortal Spirit shall never perish.
And now for you, I must work to show
the road towards the true self to unveil,

no longer in your agony to wail,
but to progress to union as you grow."

So as beloved Croton now did rise,
Myscellus that blissful unity did attain,
perceiving the infinite glory of the skies,
and no longer bound to that prior pain,
seeing all with his renewed eyes,
with joyous liberation to finally gain.

On Human Behaviour

Now in this racing digital age,
with everyone attached to their screen,
the bewildering masses I continue to gauge,
with the same human nature to be seen
since Juvenal's day, when Romans did wage
those wars on the ancient fields green,
as patterns of behaviour remain the same,
as the large majority I really must say
only strive towards each basic aim,
rather barbarian in their tedious way,
content merely with wealth and pleasure,
with more of the material to acquire,
only that which they can measure,
while their mentalities always tire.

And even with information available fast,
the majority just never take the time
to research the venerable greats past,
those minds which reached the sublime.
So many now are tragically caught
in a growing abyss of ignorance vast,
so lacking as they have only sought
all those vanities which never last.
The ignorance continues to spread,
with many not even remotely aware
of their civilization's foundation grand,
as these oblivious automatons I dread,
while so many don't appreciate nor care
for cultural achievements, always to stand,
for the immortal glories of literature and art,
for accomplishments of the human mind,
as many don't even bother to start

the crucial journey, to search and find,
to philosophize and deeply reflect,
as lower pleasures so powerfully bind,
as that vital quest I rarely detect,
while so many still wander blind.
And as suffering continues to chain,
while Time leaves them old and weak,
amidst all the fog of this plane,
still the Truth they never seek.

Serenity

Watching these wondrous birds soar
swiftly to the majestic sun high,
I sense this deep joy in my core,
this treasured serenity now as I fly.
As this radiant beauty does surround,
with devoted jubilation I must rejoice,
as the emanating glory does resound,
praising the Infinite, the Eternal voice
which truly loves and consoles each,
the caring Father who does reign,
as His splendor we all yearn to reach,
soon to journey past this painful plain
to the One which does transcend,
the immortal soul always to last,
now striving in my flight to ascend
to that revered Realm, boundlessly vast,
to the pristine bliss of that cherished land,
recalling vaguely yet longing to know,
to be free of all sorrow to withstand,
where the pure rivers endlessly flow.

The Captured Knight

There was a knight, always brave,
always dutiful on each campaign,
who now was quickly distressed to find
the enemy advancing through the plain,
joining the chaotic battle now to save
his cherished kingdom in such dread,
enduring the torment in his mind,
noticing the fallen as they bled.
Amidst the ruthless struggle fierce,
striving the onslaught to sustain,
an enemy now furiously did pierce
his open side as he fell to the ground,
shocked by the sudden, crippling pain,
as his shouts of agony did resound.

Though fortunate the clash to survive,
he was soon a prisoner and bound
to the enemy to so deeply scorn,
unable now to roam and thrive,
taken swiftly when he was found
to their dungeon as he did mourn.
Trapped in this despondent state,
he was besieged by misery's ache,
questioning the cruelty of his fate,
as existence he longed to forsake,
flooded by the sorrow which did flow,
as vicious storms with constant rain,
yearning for his freedom to know,
inundated with such despair and rage,
as his life he did completely disdain,
left in that maddening and lonely cage.
Yet after several days of this dismay,

he recalled an elder he met earlier in life,
who had spoken of an illuminating way
to move beyond all mental strife;
he lived on the kingdom's periphery far,
as he conversed with the birds which soar,
knowledgeable after many a scar,
as many wounds he also clearly bore.
He talked of journeying within and deep,
past the flux of the frenzied mind,
into the serene and cherished core,
into that wondrous bliss to truly reap,
with tranquility and love, no longer blind,
to that fortified refuge to adore;
this castle which always does stand,
though seemingly on a distant shore,
he explained was crucially close and grand,
and triumphant over that search for more,
over the restless, unfulfilled chase vain,
above all the anguish of this land,
with its radiance always to expand,
and the only source of true joy to gain.

So on this path he now did commence,
concentrating deeply for many days
on this arduous road through hours long,
understanding now the difficulty immense,
as the knight battled through the haze,
requiring all of his fortitude strong,
in the greatest battle he had ever fought,
as nothing on campaign did compare
to this grueling climb to progress past
all his voracious desires as he sought

to rise above his mind's despair,
towards that which does always last.

Now the captor came to check
on him, usually under sorrow's sway,
yet the captor was truly amazed
to see him no longer a mournful wreck;
no longer in that abyss of gloomy grey,
he was bewildered and dazed
to see the joy which did emanate
from the peaceful knight who did glow,
immersed in this harmonious state,
as his supreme serenity did flow.
He thought it useless now to keep
him imprisoned by those bars,
when suffering no longer did impede,
with his astounding bliss so deep,
and so the valiant knight was freed,
now able to see the glorious stars.

Beauty

Amidst life's painful dismay,
I saw in the wonder of her eyes
the splendor of the universe vast,
and the glory of the Infinite's way,
part of eternal beauty, always to last,
as to that serene summit I did rise,
led to silently contemplate higher
on that which manifested this world,
soaring past all my agony dire
and no longer randomly hurled
by another ruthless, perplexing gale,
but uncovering a glimmer of peace,
a harmonious calm as I did sail
while all the chaos briefly did cease,
that blissful sense only to prevail
for mere seconds and yet it did renew
with a glimpse of the fountain inside,
as that jubilant eagle swiftly flew,
its departure causing me to weep,
sensing again life's sorrow deep,
yet in my aching void she did provide
that unparalleled radiance unbound,
inspiring me so valiantly as I did ride
my true chariot, to always resound.

A Young Man

A young man, consumed by pain,
who existence did thoroughly scorn,
tired of searching through many a tome,
who was sensitive to perceive the chain,
unique in his deep suffering forlorn,
decided now boldly to venture out,
leaving his agitating and weary home,
as his perplexed family did mourn,
beyond his tedious town to scout
deep into the vast forest unknown,
as now with tenacity he did roam
in those darkening hours alone.

After walking in anguish for days,
a humble dwelling he finally found,
amidst the many towering trees,
as he approached now in his haze
this remote cabin which did astound
with its calmness amid the breeze.
And he was welcomed with grace
by the residing elder, as they did begin
a lengthy discussion, in which to trace
the young man's profound affliction within,
the constant bombardment he did face,
his dissatisfied sorrow which did spin.

And so the elder now did convey
much guidance to his beleaguered guest,
empathetic to his struggling dismay,
his distress which disrupted all rest.
"The path you must take is clear,
while your tempestuous mind does test:

you must detach from your ego dear,
and commence on that most crucial quest.
You must renounce each fleeting pleasure,
and those aspirations which only bind,
moving beyond each vain earthly treasure,
as your true core you must now find.
It can be an arduous voyage of years long,
requiring much devoted discipline austere,
but harnessing your concentration strong,
you can know that boundless bliss to revere."

"I don't want bliss, but an explanation for all
this torturing suffering which I must bear,
for this wretched existence, which is only cruel,
this vicious abyss in which we always fall,
where endless torment seems the only rule,
as this desolation continues to tear,
and sinking deeper in despair to appall,
now I must demand the reason fair!"

Another Week

I worked another grueling week
through every long, tedious hour,
while cherished rest I did seek,
the difficult labour leaving me sour;
finally the weekend did arrive
with a jubilant party to attend,
with all that food and each game,
as I laughed with every old friend
in that setting where we thrive,
immersed in those joys aflame.
Yet inevitably the party did swiftly end
and Monday morning again did call,
while each fleeting laugh did wend
its disappearing path into the cold night,
sensing the complete futility of it all,
coming down from that deceptive height,
returning once more to weary work,
to the deep emptiness and all the strife,
where this sorrow does always lurk,
tired of everything in this useless life.

The Gift of Prometheus

Endeavouring the mysteries to explain,
to myths and stories I must turn,
while we suffer intensely on this plain,
and for our freedom innately yearn.

From the Godhead there did arise
multiple beings which did emanate,
a grand hierarchy in the blissful skies,
successively emerging in their state;
yet each was more distant in its way
from the joy of the Infinite Source,
as one being, Kronos, showed dismay,
with his restless desire of much force.
And from Kronos, and his inner scourge,
his voracious longing without pause,
selfish Zeus, more flawed, then did emerge,
with even more desire which did surge,
as the material world he proudly did cause,
a world into which humanity soon fell,
trapped in the agony of this tearful life,
as our own ravenous desires always swell,
never to be satisfied through constant strife,
in this harsh desert in which we dwell.

Yet illuminating Prometheus soon did arrive,
coming down with his compassionate sight,
instructing us then with new hope to strive,
as he was gracious to bring that glorious light,
that light of inner knowledge which he taught,
the way to freedom from this cage to scorn,
as our liberation must be actively sought

by each individual in this land forlorn,
when they grow weary of this prison of pain,
and are ready to commence the work to rise
beyond the ego's desire which does stain,
as that deeper purity we must always prize,
journeying to that awareness which does beam,
towards reunion with the Godhead Supreme.

Such Hopes

Such hopes! Such hopes he had
in his prodigious youth as he did soar
with all the glorious eagles of might,
that budding boy, buoyant and glad,
as he always quested for more,
so curious with his probing sight,
unstoppable as he continued to aspire,
joyously running the length of the field,
searching for clear knowledge higher,
and never intending to yield.

But soon as he quickly grew,
a merciless illness did suddenly arrive,
viciously emerging in its stealth,
as all his hopes and ambitions flew,
ruining all his plans and his health,
left in that tortured state which did deprive
of all the opportunities he once did adore,
no longer possible to journey and thrive,
devastated to the depth of his core,
now in a vain war just to survive,
battling furiously as he did decline,
staring at the silent bewildering skies,
questioning the remote Divine,
his existence no longer to prize.

And so he then did boldly declare,
to his friends and relatives in concern,
as he was consumed by deep despair,
while all his agony continued to churn:
"My illness has enabled me to see
the essence of life on this plain,

veiled by illusory pleasures which flee,
but only dominated by mental pain,
as I've explored the vast empty haze,
while this consciousness I must disdain,
full of endless aspirations we can't reach,
with the weary succession of boring days,
each cherished ideal only to breach,
left in this lacking desert which does amaze,
with its tormenting cruelty towards each,
perplexed by this cosmos and its ways.
And love and success which we treasure
is treacherously transient if it comes at all,
and never sufficient when we measure,
impossible to fulfill us as we fall.
So don't expect anything grand
from this disappointing life here,
as we're always flooded without end
by the inevitable suffering of this land,
the storms lurking as we only steer
into the abyss as we descend."

Wandering in Reflection

Restless and anguished, I wander
again through each old, familiar street,
always compelled to excessively ponder,
while that aching void once more I meet.
Death looms for all over the fleeting field,
as the days of summer swiftly fade,
and the youthful vigor I once did wield
is tragically lost, while I can only wade
in this weariness without a crucial shield,
battling this pain which does pervade.
Now the sun disappears for the day,
only to return so tediously tomorrow,
as I'm caught under cruel agony's sway,
with another Monday morning to dread,
where behind each laugh insincere
there's a vast desert of deep sorrow,
as life's inexorable end I still fear,
while the grief continues to spread,
noticing now an elderly couple frail,
who back to their home slowly tread,
illness destroying the body, fated to fail,
as existence weaves its tragic thread.

After all our grand struggle and toil,
the beloved connections gained,
all our achievements on this soil,
all the growth and wisdom attained,
surely the Infinite Absolute will save
the preciously cherished individual soul,
after such suffering we did brave,
progressing onward to the goal.
And yet personal individuality may be

only temporary, even on a higher plane,
as we are meant finally to know and see,
after the many lives of the arduous chain,
to finally unite with the Supreme,
to be completely limitless and free,
to be one with boundless Brahman High,
where endless bliss does always teem,
ultimately merging with the Godhead to fly,
the Source from which all does beam,
transcending all pain which does stream,
eternal consciousness beyond the sky.
Yet each individual soul which did roam
surely Brahman still must always know,
recalling the long course of each back home,
back to those fountains of joy which flow,
and so even in that one united state,
nothing must be lost of each soul's glory,
that expressive evolution towards its fate,
and the path of every personal story.
And yet I'm still in this constant pain,
with this dire desolation to appall,
which my energy continues to drain,
as I still continue to question all:
the purpose of these wanderings here
amidst all these hardships without end,
enduring these battles always near,
as the night now does descend.
Unique is my individual discontent,
the labyrinth of my distressed mind,
with the complexity of my afflicted state,
that colossal chasm which does torment,
to which no one can truly relate,
with no complete understanding to find,
and so I walk back now in the cold,

amid this drowning loneliness immense,
with the immeasurable universe to behold,
still perplexed in my pensive sense.

Yet I see now this fleeting owl of speed,
and I'm reminded of Minerva of yore,
as I recall my jubilant youth when I did read
of the Greeks and Romans to adore,
and all those ancient seekers of might,
who some of the darkness did dispel,
constantly probing with their valiant sight,
questioning this world in which we dwell.
And suddenly I see the convergence clear,
with a flash of wondrous joy to cherish,
between Platonists and Vedantists to revere,
and all the great mystics of East and West,
with their mighty legacy never to perish,
united on that common, devoted quest,
those venerable sages I'll always admire,
while in this tempestuous abyss I steer,
as I'm energized now with thoughts higher,
with this new radiance in my aching core,
rejuvenated with greater hope dear,
and yearning so deeply to soar.

In the Cavern

He was trapped for many years
in a dire cavern, dreary and dark,
weakening in complete dismay,
as piercing pain did constantly mark
his bewildering days of decay,
struggling to battle his fears,
as he continued in silence to pray,
in anguish through his solitary tears.

In his restlessness he did stir,
as furious flames continued to churn,
always with that agony to endure,
that dreaded fire always to spurn,
as only this relentless fire he did sense,
left in his boundless misery to burn,
in this excruciating blaze immense,
while for his freedom he did yearn.

He continued to descend and sink,
destroyed by each attack severe,
approaching his threshold's brink,
and unable to keep his hopes dear.
Yet shockingly he then did meet
an ancestor wise who did appear,
with such compassion as he did greet,
as his presence he did so revere,
as the ancestor then did remind,
offering his calm words serene,
inspiring his beleaguered mind,
turning him back to the fields green.

"But truly you are not the fire,
and all the pain which does scar.
You must with fortitude aspire,
no longer identifying with the blaze;
greater than that you are,
beyond all this illusory haze.
Within there is a fountain pure,
which always does gloriously flow,
endlessly tranquil and secure,
and towards this fountain I will show,
beyond all your agony and cries,
purifying in peace as you grow,
and beyond the fire you shall rise,
meant those joyful waters to know."

The King and His Advisor

There was a certain ancient King,
who impressive power did command,
who would often turn to and call
on his astute advisor who would bring
his various views and guidance grand
for the betterment of his reign,
as the ardent King would never stall
his realm's growth, as he did obtain
much pleasure in his drive to expand,
always eyeing the distant plain.

As the mighty King continued to yearn
for more glory, in his voracious trance,
this old advisor, prudent and stern,
now surprised the ruler with his stance.
"I advise you a noble temple to raise,
to stand with its inspiring height,
its striking radiance to always amaze,
bringing your people to sacred ground,
and illuminating with its endless light,
its everlasting wonder to resound.
Its construction should truly take
urgent precedence now in its way,
greater than every other prize,
with all other campaigns to forsake,
proceeding ahead without delay,
as you are meant to know the skies,
concentrating intensely as you pray,
labouring and finding your inner eyes,
sacrificing your time until that day,
when your temple will finally rise."

"That is absurd. What will I gain
by building a temple in my land?
I have many aspirations to attain,
and several useful structures planned.
And I must further work to train
my men for battle as they defend
my cherished kingdom, never to wane,
into new frontiers soon to send,
as I must now labour and seek
my beloved cities to extend,
continuing with speed to grow,
never to diminish, never weak,
but as a great river to always flow,
gaining new territory as I strive,
never daunted by storms, nor snow,
enjoying the fruits as I will thrive."

So the King continued without concern
for the words of this advisor old,
as to his numerous ambitions he did turn,
dedicated to his dear kingdom to mold.
And with his talents he did excel,
as his flourishing rule many did admire,
as his vast domain did quickly swell,
confronting his enemies in battle's fire,
with new victories on each foreign field,
celebrating the triumphs he did earn,
relishing in the dominance he did wield,
while his hopes continued to churn.
New cities he then proudly did found,
with his soaring prosperity to savor,

as he felt that he was never bound,
open to new possibilities immense,
all progressing in his favour,
with all of life's pleasures to sense.
Yet even with all this surging might,
the King still felt a distressing hole,
a piercing dissatisfaction to always fight,
a certain emptiness beyond control,
as he was restless through each night,
still chasing each coveted goal.
So his advisor he again did pursue,
while this interior chasm perilously grew.
"I'm still not satisfied, full of dismay,
even with all my achievements great,
as I sense this relentless grey,
always ravaged by this state.
I'm able rival kingdoms to defeat,
yet I can never vanquish this pain,
never content with my high seat,
as I'm plagued by this endless bane,
impossible all my desires to meet,
as this grief I must disdain."

"I see the angst in your eyes,
yet you never bothered to proceed
to build the temple as I did advise,
as only your hunger you did feed,
while neglecting my insights wise,
with your voracious hunger the seed
for all your suffering and cries,
as your desires will always exceed
your desperate reach and hold,
as you are left now in this aching cold."

The King's rising rage then did erupt
as a furious volcano as he did scold
his poor advisor, sending him away,
far into dismal exile, a decision abrupt,
confident in his own knowledge bold,
as he no longer permitted him to stay.
"Your presence I can no longer bear,
no longer in need of your senile thought,
as it is you who will endure the frozen air,
in the remote winds to be caught."

So the King continued with his strength,
resuming the expansion of his domain,
and his growing populace did often exalt
as he governed for many years in length,
always enlarging his treasury's vault
and planning his next lofty campaign.
And he persisted despite that inner ache,
focusing on the next high ambition,
with so many intricate strategies to make,
zealous with his every mission.

Yet eventually a faction in his court
grew envious of his mounting power,
as they gathered to eagerly prepare,
waiting for the opportune hour
to strike and the King's reign tear,
as to insurrection they did resort.
The sudden revolt swiftly did turn
to the destructive horror of civil strife,
as several buildings did quickly burn
in the escalation of the tragic fight,
with the King fearing for his life,

and pacing in the dread of the night.
Lacking sufficient soldiers loyal,
eventually he was forced to run,
losing his treasured palace royal,
fleeing as all the traitors did stun,
overthrown, as another did replace,
now outside his kingdom in lament,
out in the wilderness in disgrace,
and still shocked by the dissent.

He wandered then for many days,
unable to fathom his swift decline,
immersed in his miserable haze,
as he often questioned the Divine.
And in his humbled position low,
his former advisor he then did find,
surprised to see him with his glow,
while he fought his anguished mind,
moving closer as he did see
the man's smile from afar,
as he seemed peaceful and free,
and calm as a steadfast star.

"O my old advisor and guide,
I was too rash, always seeking more,
full of such towering, arrogant pride,
as I've lost everything I did adore;
as fast as the fleeting birds they flew
and now my life I can only deplore,
with only increasing agony to accrue,
now battling within this brutal war."

"To enrich your kingdom you sought,
but you never enriched your core,
never pursuing any higher thought,
but always another remote shore.
Yet as you endure your woes vast,
as you have so painfully lost all,
you are really in a position now to gain
that which shall always truly last,
that which soars beyond this plain,
as you can still climb that peak tall."

"But that temple I can't build now,
lacking the treasury and each resource,
as the skies seem only to endow
such sinking sorrow on my course."

"Yet there is really no reason to weep,
as truly the temple is actually inside,
and all that majestic splendor is deep,
its blissful glory never to subside."

In this Lonely Forest

Deep in this lonely forest dire,
I'm so far from the one I cherish,
always ravaged by this ruthless fire,
as I find myself longing to perish;
unattainable she always does remain,
so distant from those glorious eyes,
as I only sense now more disdain
for this desolate and lowly land,
still questioning the indifferent skies,
which force me as a prisoner to sustain,
constantly this emptiness to withstand,
as I yearn to flee this distressing plane,
to transcend all my agony and rise,
and finally break through every chain
which holds me in this cruel cell,
so weary of this material domain,
always isolated from the one I adore,
no longer to hear that youthful bell,
always besieged in my battered core,
as the sorrow continues to swell.

Often wandering as I lament,
in a wretched cave at night I dwell,
questioning merciless nature's intent,
while I'm nostalgic for that prior age,
that era of elation before I fell,
yet this existence is now a cage,
consciousness continuing to torment,
while I search desperately for a sage,
for a person of wisdom to assist,
yet we live in a period of decline,
a material epoch of nihilistic mist,

where even the knowledgeable few
don't know the depth of the Divine,
as all the venerable seers flew,
and I'm left on my own to discern,
against this darkness to defend,
while the harsh winds often churn,
searching for precious clarity alone,
yearning to finally understand,
to unveil the bewildering unknown,
and uncover my essence grand.
And all those illusory joys of old
I can no longer value nor revere,
as only the Infinite I must behold,
all else merely a stubborn veneer,
the Infinite truly the only source
of that bliss which will always last,
meant to voyage on with force,
towards that greater harmony vast.

But separated from the lady I treasure,
how can I really endure this sense
of devastation beyond all measure,
my kingdom in these ruins to decry,
observing all the carnage immense,
and the destruction of my castles high?
So here in this vicious forest dark,
alone amidst these dying trees,
my solitary footsteps continue to mark
my purposeless path without a goal,
with everything as fleeting as the breeze,
as I only sink further in this horrid hole,
which now seems boundless in its way,

destroying my very being weak,
with the radiance so remote in dismay,
while I question if I should even seek,
left to face another crippling day
here in this endless wilderness bleak.

Towards Knowledge: A Vision

I was wandering for days,
anguished and isolated from all,
weary through the remote plain,
deeply immersed in a foggy haze,
with my cries for help, each call
unanswered through all my pain,
towards the cruel sky as I would gaze,
in that aching abyss as I did fall.

Then a humble hermitage I did find,
approaching this curious dwelling old,
ready my loneliness now to heal,
to converse with a wise mind,
with some loftier thoughts to mold,
as I was tired of the agonizing wheel,
the tedious repetition of dismay,
all the sorrow of unfulfilled desire,
ready for a new road, a different way,
to gain freedom from the fierce fire.

So I questioned the hermit inside,
hoping that this noble elder would guide:
"Why this painful voyage? Why am I here?
Why this perplexing universe which grew?
I turn to you now with reverence dear:
What really is my nature true?"

"My friend, there is a certain cave
which you must work now to reach,
as you must always remain brave,
your defenses never to breach.
For the path is arduous and long,
and many are not ready in this life,

as your concentration must be strong,
as you endure the recurring strife."

So towards this cave I moved ahead,
as the hermit's words did enthrall,
still in fatigue as I then did tread,
yet finding new zeal, never to stall.
And uncovering the cave, I did descend
deep into that cold and misty lair,
through the rocks, turning the bend,
and further into that darkness to bear.
There was desolation without end,
as vast emptiness I did sense,
bewildered by the path he did send,
as I faced that hole immense.
Then I was surprised by a shine,
as I reached my hand to the ground,
and in the soil which did entwine,
a wondrous lyre there I found.

Leaving the cave, another was there,
waiting for me as he did greet,
an old man with a radiant smile,
emanating such compassion and care,
introducing himself as we did meet,
explaining further as he did beguile.

"I am a reclusive prophet, a seer,
as this great land I often roam;
today is a day to truly revere,
as you are now closer to your home.
I saw with such clarity years prior,
your entrance into that cave,
knowing that you would find that lyre,
its boundless glory which will save.

Now that lyre you must provide
as a crucial offering without delay,
to the nearby temple wide,
where in devotion you will stay."

So after this prophet did confide,
I walked to this temple grand,
uplifted with an ardent stride,
as my soaring energies did expand.
Those majestic columns I saw,
as I humbly approached near,
the temple leaving me in such awe,
illuminated by the Sun so clear.

Within a priest then did address,
noticing all my fatigue and distress:
"Your suffering has brought you here,
with your deep yearning to be free,
as on a sacred route you now steer,
striving towards Truth, to finally see.
To the One, I will show you the way,
with that inner knowledge to attain,
beyond even the highest skies,
in concentration as you must pray,
as you purify beyond every stain,
with the Infinite the only prize,
sternly renouncing all that is vain,
our common destiny to gloriously rise.
The eternal wisdom I shall share,
as glorious union you shall realize,
that unity which is already there,
pervading all and throughout the air,
as you will remove the stubborn veil,
voyaging towards that blessed shore,
with knowledge to finally prevail,

ready to reach the Spirit in your core,
the bliss which always does reign,
the Truth triumphant on your course,
to be liberated from this aching plain,
soon to return to the Ultimate Source."

The Kingdom

There was a glorious kingdom grand,
one kingdom in which all did unite,
the immense union with its plentiful land,
as all the joyful inhabitants did thrive,
reaching in their joy that majestic height,
in common fellowship as they did strive,
savoring the peace of that long reign,
serene in the security of that might,
never burdened by sorrow's stain,
in the splendor of that beaming light.

Yet eventually many then did seek
to venture into the vast unknown,
compelled to separate and leave,
to explore the rough wilderness alone,
open to vulnerabilities and weak,
yet with many possibilities to perceive.
So numerous principalities small
quickly began to emerge and grow,
relishing in their independent way,
as their countless ambitions did flow,
eager to defend with each wall,
each rising castle with its sway,
as fierce rivalries then did appall,
with the threat of battle each day.
Several achievements of renown
many individuals did proudly attain,
with the principalities toiling to expand,
developing from each modest town,
with more influence as they did stand,
augmenting their power on the plain,
always questing zealously for more,

dedicated to their cherished domain,
labouring towards the next shore,
for their next aspiration to gain.

Many however did eventually sense
a certain weariness which grew,
and an aching chasm of pain intense,
as their treasured youth swiftly flew,
as there was a surging desire to be free
of that perplexing agony to bear,
tormenting as a tempestuous sea,
as they then longed for that calmer air.
So they decided with courage to depart
from their cities and all they did adore,
yearning deeply with each ardent heart
to really fulfill their deepest core,
as their lands they bravely left behind,
never satisfied with that restless life,
changing the focus of their mind,
and hoping to soar past all their strife.

Commencing on that arduous road,
that long walk through forests and snow,
they longed for their true abode,
the one realm which was always there,
finding the glory which they all did share,
their old kingdom once again to know.

The Search

The Genoese sailor in his distress
now a local resident did address:
"I've searched through your city sublime
for my cherished Caterina, my beloved fair,
treasuring the glory of our lost time,
longing to see her in my deep despair.
We met near the mountains high,
as we both yearned to explore,
quickly enamoured as we did fly,
as majestic birds inspired to soar.
Together in our jubilation Divine,
blessed with euphoria from above,
her marvelous eyes did stunningly shine,
as we were united in wondrous love,
her splendor reaching triumphant height,
radiant with her unsurpassed light,
but then that dreadful war did erupt
between our two rival states bold,
so tragic as it then did disrupt,
clashing again with battles to behold:
Genoa challenging your Venice of might,
with the dread of that ominous hour,
competing for dominance in the fight,
and always zealous for more power.

The conflict then did separate,
losing my lady in such dismay,
as I questioned mysterious fate,
recalling the grief of that horrid day.
Taken away so swiftly after we met,
her father clearly sought to protect
young Caterina from the war's threat,
from the dangers he did expect.

So in the rough sea I then fought,
serving dutifully in our gallant fleet,
as the tactical advantage we sought,
with many grave perils to meet.
But now that the war did cease,
free from fierce combat's rage,
finally grateful for the relief of peace,
as our vessels no longer engage,
I'm searching for my Caterina here,
flooded my such sorrowful fear
that I will never again gaze
upon those beaming celestial eyes,
truly unequalled in her ways,
her brilliance to always prize."

Now sympathetic to his cry,
the Venetian was quick to reply:
"Of this Caterina I did certainly hear,
with her great beauty widely known,
even admired by the mighty throne,
the Doge among many who do revere.
After the war, I know she did depart
and with her father they did steer
towards the Greek islands to chart,
on a certain mission for Venice dear.
But unfortunately as we grieve,
their galley never did return,
likely shipwrecked as I believe,
yet impossible to truly discern."

"Neptune's seas can be unkind,
as the storms many ships have blown,
yet my Caterina I'm determined to find,
not willing to leave her lost and alone;
I truly believe in my soul deep

that she still must be alive,
probably in pain as she does weep,
working with resilience to survive."

Resolute with tenacious force,
now to the Greek islands on his way,
he resumed his searching course,
swiftly ahead without delay.
Driven by his lasting love pure,
with all his ardor and strength,
he still had to toil to endure
his arduous journey of length,
with the perilous waters to traverse,
reaching many islands to survey,
concerned with the winds adverse,
and hostile ships looking for prey.
So through many a difficult night,
her stunning smile he did recall,
striving to muster more might,
as the rains did often fall.

But after much time at sea,
after so many islands to scout,
though praying with many a plea,
he now felt such rising doubt,
as he more intensely did fear
that he would never again be near
angelic Caterina to so venerate,
always to adore her soul dear,
burdened now by much weight,
unable to bear his solitary state,
left in his agonizing dismay,
his greatest days perhaps past,
sailing under the weary skies grey,
wandering in the lonely waters vast.

Though he was aching and weak,
facing his anguished pain deep,
he continued with persistence to seek,
his precious hope still to keep,
and so as he did persevere,
as a climber to that new height,
finally the fog began to clear
and in the distance he did sight
a massive Cross which did stand,
calling him now to pursue and land.
And on this compelling island he found
a church and monastery great,
as rejoicing choirs did resound,
sensing the workings of fate;
here a welcoming monk he did greet,
who seemed a gift from the higher sky,
grateful this pious man to meet,
as to his questions he did caringly reply.

"Yes, a wrecked vessel we did find,
which made its way recently ashore,
which troubled many a mind,
as I was shocked in my core
when only one survivor did emerge,
after that storm's mighty force,
a fortunate lady enduring the scourge,
persisting through its course.
With her injuries, many an ache,
facing all her grief and pain,
into our care we then did take,
nourishing her as we did sustain."

From the monastery, he then did bring
glorious Caterina into the sun,
hearing all the cosmos then sing,

as her beauty again did stun.
And the two in joyful tears
in such elation did then embrace,
triumphant over all their fears,
and relinquishing every trace
of old doubt and disdain,
reborn with deeper sight,
with ecstatic bliss to attain,
truly blessed to finally reunite,
rejuvenated as they did gain
an ocean of boundless light,
as their eternal souls did align
with that lasting love Divine.

Besieged

Existence always attacks in its way
with its cruel onslaught fierce,
constantly bombarding each day,
as the endless siege does pierce
my crumbling defenses weak,
with all my grueling efforts vain,
condemned to this struggle bleak
and no longer able to sustain,
as I'm forced to battle in this cold,
while my diminishing energies drain,
with this life to furiously scold,
with my battered walls coming down,
forsaking the hope I once did keep
and decaying in strength as I wane,
left here seemingly only to weep,
alone against these armies of renown,
and immersed so painfully deep
in this sorrow in which I drown.

And then when I'm on the ground,
convinced that I can bear no more,
existence only continues to pound,
still vicious as it devastates my core,
as my unheard screams resound
on this remote and isolated shore,
here in this punishing, barren land,
which is miserably bereft of light,
this wretched wilderness, lacking fruit,
where each hour I must withstand,
while lacking that clarity of sight
against enemy hordes and each brute,
always exhausted by this labour weary,

still assailed by that tyrannical court,
as I carry these heavy stones dreary
to reinforce again my shattered fort.

Submerged in this emptiness vast,
which everything does pervade,
impossible in this agony to last,
I'm utterly bewildered as I fade,
and I long for some peace serene,
while I'm unable even briefly to rest,
amidst the dying trees, no longer green,
as the ruthless assault continues to test
the extent of my resilience and might,
as soon my threshold I will surely reach,
tasked with an unreachable height,
and soon to suffer that critical breach.
So in this merciless war without end,
always enduring this agonizing lack,
further into the desolation I descend,
sinking deeper into the vile void black,
impossible this misery to transcend,
as I await the next dreaded attack.

The Old Exile

The crew of explorers, long at sea,
decided to investigate, as they did land
on an intriguing island, remote and small,
with its vegetation thick, many a tree,
as the captain with his decoration grand
led his veteran crew, motioning to all
to quicken their pace into the forest deep,
as they then found, lying under the shade,
this old man in pain, as he did appall,
while the nearby trees all did weep
for this beleaguered elder as he did fade,
the observing crew now all dismayed.

"Old man, you look unwell
on this distant island unknown,
far from a familiar town bell,
with only birds to hear you groan,
as the heat continues to swell,
yet why are you here alone?"

"I was exiled, so sudden and cruel,
to this miserable island quickly sent,
impossible to comprehend his rule,
so long beset by all this torment.
I was brought to this dread years prior
and forced to endure on my own,
surviving in this wretched condition dire,
as existence I can only bemoan,
completely immersed in the ruthless fire,
while the winds have so swiftly blown
all my hopes, each vanishing leaf,
as I watched my fragile health decline,

falling further into this boundless hole,
as I must question the enigmatic Divine,
plunging into a black chasm of grief,
with my endless agony, that constant toll,
lacking a clear and decisive sign
in this barren life, only brutal and brief.

Trapped in this solitary state,
the relentless loneliness did tear
my very being, furious at my fate,
such loneliness impossible to bear.
To the abyss I've always been bound,
as the merciless waves the island crash,
with sweet freedom never to be found,
fighting a war every day, each clash,
with that sense of death all around,
as a destroyed city in ruins and decay,
while the enemy continues to surround,
leaving me battered in disarray.
And the abyss has become part
of my nature as I must declare,
without any purpose here to chart,
while my scorn pervades the air.
How much pain can a man take
before he finally reaches the brink,
before this life he must finally forsake,
left always in distress to sink?"

Astounded by his calamitous cry,
and hoping to see the elder restored,
the captain in sympathy did reply,
eager to take him now aboard.
"We would be glad to take you back,

away from this isolation here
and all this lament and lack,
back to your previous home dear."

"There is no land which I consider home,
in this wearisome world to deplore,
with sorrow regardless of where I roam,
with this intrinsic suffering to abhor.
And it is really too late now to leave,
as I am already in sickness severe,
sensing very short, fleeting time left,
as I've been ravaged without reprieve,
grateful for my departure to finally steer
away from this world of affliction bereft.
This excruciating existence is only pain,
as the cruel gods I don't understand,
struggling so long to survive and maintain,
with the excessive anguish to withstand,
and all the exhausting labour on this plain,
toiling so intensely merely to stand.
Yet for what? Was my long endurance bold
a notable victory of some kind to praise?
This is only a useless life I must scold,
dying in the blazing heat of the sun's rays,
enraged against being itself which does mold
ceaseless torture in an infinite myriad of ways.

In my younger years, before my exile,
I talked to a certain man wise,
as I already sensed life's brutality vile,
probing for some clarity in his eyes.
We are all Divine, as he would explain,
all part of that one infinite Mind,
yet our obscured view does stain,
as we often walk these paths blind.

But unable to confirm, I always did remain
in the unknown, never able to unwind
the harsh ignorance which does chain,
which breeds that desolation of the kind
which renders all a meaningless bane,
without any saving solace to find.
If there is indeed an infinite Source,
then why this universe did it manifest,
forcing upon us this agonizing course,
the suffering of this anguished quest?
Why did we really have to emerge,
arising and struggling in this troubled form,
battling vicious emotions, every scourge,
always to face each ruthless storm?

Some nights when loneliness did consume,
as vast as the cosmos at which I did gaze,
as I longed so zealously for the tomb,
in the insignificance of my misty daze,
so alone in the universe then I felt,
crushed by the silence which did befall,
and everything so swiftly did melt
into the horrid nothingness of all."

Towards the Palace: A Vision

Filled with fiery fury which long did boil,
a valiant army I swiftly did form,
my massive legion, daring and loyal,
eager the harsh tyrant to finally storm,
that vicious King with his ruthless reign,
overseeing with his power such dismay,
the vast suffering and excessive pain,
the populace always weary of his way,
as an ardent following I now did attain,
no longer willing in our agony to delay,
deploring the desolation in his domain,
and all the torment which did abound,
ready to overthrow his torturous rule,
foreseeing complete victory to gain,
the glory of that triumphant sound
and the end of his despotism cruel.

So we set out on our way ahead,
towards the King, so remotely far,
fighting against all our fear and dread,
and already battered with many a scar,
striving on our exhausting march long
across that arduous and vast land,
only suited for the resilient and strong,
as we moved closer to his home grand,
needing then that intrepid climb high,
ascending that majestic yet perilous peak,
as his fortifications seemed in the sky,
while his daunting palace we did seek.
Then finding that level ground,
we finally reached his walls of might,
in awe of his defenses to behold,

as his formidable authority did resound,
his royal citadel an impressive sight,
amazed at everything he did mold,
with his protected palace at that height
so heavily guarded as we did scold
his uncaring regime, his power profound,
his throne responsible for all our plight,
which kept us to aching misery bound,
but only emboldened our will to fight.

His alarmed army now did emerge,
swiftly confronting us outside,
as I expected that guarding force,
with rising rage as we did converge,
yet I had greater numbers on my side,
with many tired of the King's course,
as we were ready to end the scourge,
with focused purpose as we did ride.
Many of my dedicated men did fall,
with the constant clashing of each sword,
facing much anguished doubt,
as the intensity of combat did appall,
yet soon I was exhilarated to shout
with victory over that savage horde,
ready now to breach that towering wall,
to besiege the citadel which did protect,
never intending on our path to stall,
even as more defenders we did detect
flooding out again to attempt to shield
the King's stronghold which stood so tall,
while all that blood stained the field,
hearing each desperate yell and call.

My large crew of engineers brave
had been building siege weapons behind
the line of combat as they did prepare
to unleash our bombardment, each wave
of crucial ferocity through the air,
as each precious catapult did unwind.
And as our attacks continued to swell,
his imposing walls could not sustain,
as his entire crumbling citadel fell,
his great defenses no longer to maintain,
leaving him vulnerable as we did pour
into his cherished city, venturing deep
amid all those structures he did adore,
as jubilant confidence we now did reap,
fighting off the last guards without concern
and advancing with swift pace to his core,
as my objective I intended to keep,
towards his palace as I long did yearn.

Ready the enigmatic leader to meet,
immersed in the bewildering unknown,
I approached his grand structure with awe,
now entering the King's palace alone,
walking up to the grandeur of his seat,
as the King himself I finally saw,
now with the momentous chance
to question and to boldly address
this old monarch and now advance
my disdain for all the kingdom's distress,
the distress which this ruler did cause,
permitting all our sorrow immense,
which plagues us without pause,
abandoning us in the abyss immense.

"You who this miserable kingdom built,
who all this cruel suffering did create,
in which everything does wane and wilt,
leaving us to this excruciating fate:
it is unacceptable as I must declare,
which led me to reach your estate,
while excessive pain the multitudes bear,
as I long now to be free of this state."

"I'm very impressed with your strength,
with the tenacious focus of your pursuit,
enduring all those perils of length,
as your efforts I must now salute.
No one has reached me in years,
here in my palace on the peak,
yet you dare to question the tears,
the nature of that which seems bleak.
Yet the true King is higher than me,
with an even greater palace sublime,
wondrous and glorious without end,
as I can teach you now to see,
as it is now the appropriate time,
with all of your pain to transcend.
And when that supreme palace you find,
you will no longer need to return
to this land which torments the mind,
free of this lower desert which you spurn.
Then you shall finally live in peace,
where serenity as a fountain does flow,
with exultant joy never to cease,
and your radiance always to glow."

The Elder of the Mountain

There was a noble elder of endless age,
who dwelled on his cherished, majestic peak,
who carried the calmness of a knowing sage,
beyond all the lower, arduous plains so bleak,
as he was immersed in joy which did teem,
boundless bliss which did gloriously resound,
greater than the countless stars as they beam,
long secure in that serene state profound.

And yet after so many jubilant years,
he eventually developed aspirations new,
the desire for individual experience bold,
even recognizing the inevitability of tears,
with the desire to play, to love and create,
as all these surging ambitions then grew,
energized by the new possibilities to mold,
and ready to depart from his revered home,
to leave behind his native, tranquil state,
and descend to the many fields to roam.

So down the grand mountain he came,
from that one peak he long did adore,
with all his myriad yearnings to tame,
to pursue now each crucial ambition,
with seemed to rise from his aching core
as fierce creatures in a once restful sea,
traversing with hunger towards each mission,
and labouring with the multitudes diverse,
among the various leaves of a growing tree,
ardently dedicated to strive and achieve,
with flourishing efforts as he did immerse,
eager for the opportunities he did perceive.

For many years his life did satisfy,
even gaining recognition for his work,
content to be a traveller under the sky,
always pressing onward for more,
yet a certain agitation then began to lurk,
a certain distressing cavern to endure,
with flooding rains waiting to pour,
as those old winds began to stir.
And though he was able to thrive,
experiencing and accomplishing with skill,
towards the numerous shores to arrive,
creating uniquely as he did aspire,
after much time he ultimately did find
that nothing in this land could really fill,
perceiving a new agony in his mind,
and amid this growing anguish dire
an enormous abyss he did sense,
no longer concerned with his old desire,
but only trapped in emptiness immense.

Weary of the intrinsically painful land,
with all its misery he did deplore,
he could no longer now withstand,
isolating himself in introspection intense,
with a deep longing to triumphantly soar,
as he decided then to commence
his courageous climb, turning back,
as he yearned for his peak to return,
to be free of all that aching lack,
of all those storms which did churn.
So driven with devotion to ascend
and reach the mountain's glorious height,

as an inspired chariot of renewed force,
with his inner essence to work to mend,
focusing his resilient energies and might,
he was ready now to face and brave
all the long perils of his solitary course,
knowing that only the mountain could save.
Compelled by that rising inner call,
beyond the plain's sorrowful torment,
guided by that harmonious sound,
devoted on his trek and never to stall,
towards the summit's radiance he went,
that immeasurable radiance vast,
where the serenity does truly abound,
towards his joyful home to reunite,
where the bliss does always last,
with the birds in their wondrous flight.

To Endure

The exhausted group, immersed in toil,
working under the fierce heat of the Sun,
had been condemned to cruel labour for life,
and confined on this miserable soil,
aching in the anguish of ceaseless strife,
without their freedom, impossible to run,
with all the King's guards in their place,
serving that tyrant who did viciously declare
this brutal sentence of labour to face,
claiming that these former soldiers did fare
too poorly in the latest battle of defense
against their furious rival in the latest war,
sending them to this descending despair,
a capricious punishment to deplore,
when they had actually been quite strong,
serving the kingdom in that crisis immense
with great courage through the peril long,
performing with skill in the combat intense,
yet the proud King was eager to reprimand,
exerting again his dominating power,
forcing this lowly group now to withstand
all the torment of each excruciating hour.
Pushing each heavy brick and stone,
pressed through the endless work,
they were never given enough rest,
while all their prior hopes had flown,
as these vast building projects did test
all their resilience, as the pain did lurk,
always torturing their gloomy days,
left in the desolate drudgery distressed,
and only living now in a dark haze,
despising the old King and his crest.
One of the weary labourers weak,

turning to the other men in the cold,
in his cosmic sorrow now did speak,
as his furious lament he did mold.
"Confronting all this constant pain,
I only long now for sweet death,
to finally flee this devastating plain,
as I wait for my escape, my last breath.
This is really a useless life we lead,
always trapped in this desolate cage,
while the King continues to expand
all his grand luxuries in voracious greed,
while I'm consumed by rising rage,
despising this world, this wretched land.
Each dreaded day is just another attack
of this merciless and perpetual pain to bear,
as precious liberty we crucially lack,
and now in this futility I no longer care
about this dismal life, reaching my brink,
suffering excessively as we weep,
as I continue in my agony to sink
into this vile nothingness deep."

Another labourer now did turn,
ready his fellow prisoner to address,
sensing the flames which did burn,
united in their common distress.
"We suffer, yet bravely we endure
through all these days of dismay,
with the sanctuary of our core pure,
finding now the fortitude to stay,
to stay strong through every ache,
holding to that beaming inner ray,
which fortifies through the long fight,
as our hope we shall never forsake,
bracing each new storm on our way,

and rejuvenating with endless might,
our essence impossible to break,
always able to cherish our light.
Our castles they can never defeat,
as we shall valiantly maintain,
keeping the honour of our seat,
with our boundless spirit to sustain,
as knights of glory as we hold,
truly impossible to ever chain,
our endurance a triumph to behold,
with all our efforts never in vain.
We shall struggle on with strength,
even as the winds continue to stir;
through all these trials of length,
we suffer, yet bravely we endure."

The Search for Saturn

I was with a venerable ancient seer,
who in the mighty Alps did dwell,
as I had voyaged a long way
finally with this elder to be near,
my deep pain continuing to swell,
immersed in my anguished dismay,
while this astute man I did so revere,
who had lived for countless years,
even before we tragically fell,
when we flourished without tears;
so in my weariness I began to express
all my dissatisfaction and distress.

"His ruthless reign continues to astound,
leaving us in this emptiness vile,
swamped by all this sorrow profound,
while he subjects us to this wretched trial:
of that torturing tyrant Jupiter I speak,
furious with his ways, always cruel,
while we swiftly decline, so weak,
so bewildered by his merciless rule.
He wants us to experience pain,
with such suffering in order to advance,
to adapt and develop through woes,
as we're struck by each agonizing lance,
forced to endure this desolate plane,
as his system I can only oppose,
necessary to take this bold stance,
while all the sick in their misery cry,
while we're enslaved on this barren soil,
always to question that harsh sky,
as we're trapped in this tiring toil,
the land always needing more work,

impossible to this despot to be loyal,
while all the torment always does lurk,
the torment of consciousness in this mode,
with disappointment's constant stain,
carrying each burden's exhausting load,
and left with all this deepening disdain."

"With all my empathy I truly understand,
as ignorant Jupiter is a cruel ruler indeed,
a regent with many flaws which flow,
as he watches us struggle on this land;
it is tragic that he now does lead,
as the Infinite Source he doesn't know,
the true Spirit which did manifest,
which this universe and all did project.
Yet when we're able to creatively express,
thriving at that optimal peak best,
with those resounding joys to detect,
no longer in that tedium and stress,
we are linked to the expression Divine
of the One, the Infinite Energy High,
which limited personhood is above,
which needs no sacrifice nor shrine,
able to rise as the jubilant birds fly,
with a glorious bliss beyond even love,
as each inspired individual lyre,
with endless imagination unbound,
is part of that one chorus Higher,
the wonder of that harmonious sound,
manifesting in these myriad ways,
that one forest of limitless trees,
truly united through all our days
to the glory of those boundless seas."

In my agitation I then did reply,
sensing only a fruitless desert dry,
"But now, chained to labour to survive,
there is so little time to fully pursue
the glory of art, as the weary days deprive
me of my calling, my mission true,
which then only adds to the anguish,
my discontent only to increase,
tired of the mundane as I languish,
and churning without cherished peace."

"Even as your fleeting time is short,
towards the sublime you still must strive,
as the refuge of art is your sacred fort
against the tyranny of this vicious life,
as it will sustain you, keeping you alive
amid all the recurring tempests of strife,
as to ecstatic Eternity it is your link,
to reach that tranquility when you stir,
returning to that fountain of joy to drink,
to those everlasting waters pure.
Now back in the age of Saturn's reign,
humanity was elated and free,
with an abundance of food for all,
and no miserable labour to drain,
with never an old nor dying tree,
as each could pursue their call,
their chosen vocation uniquely bold,
as the fields were then full of song,
with such serenity as all did mold
in that time of such euphoria strong,
unburdened by the pain you scold,
the beaming Sun radiant so long.
It was a time of knowledge wide,
when each their Divinity knew,

our unity with the Infinite Source,
without this current egoistic pride,
when each to majestic heights flew,
with never a wandering course.
But now in this chaotic present age,
so many are sadly unaware,
in that dreary and dark cage,
with many destroyed by despair,
as the covetous masses are vain,
consumed by each insatiable desire,
devoid of artistic appreciation and sense,
forgetting Beauty's origin as they wane,
sinking into nihilistic nothingness dire,
and left with that aching hole immense."

"But how can I work to properly return
beloved Saturn to his rightful throne,
to restore that golden age as I yearn,
and reinstate that triumphant tone?
Wearied of the raging fires which burn,
I long for that knowledge complete,
no longer with this suffering to spurn,
but that lasting joy to finally meet."

"Saturn is chained on an island remote,
imprisoned in a forsaken cave deep,
with the location sorrowfully unknown,
with his lamentations as he does weep;
yet you must search for him by boat,
even through all the hazards which await,
even if you must travel for years alone,
in order to finally free him from his state,
so that he can challenge Jupiter once more,
rejuvenated as he again must rise,
with no more agony in your battered core,

as he must retake his place in the skies.
Now with grand fortitude and strength,
your ardent search you must commence,
continuing to strive through every storm,
enduring your vital voyage of length,
dedicated as you maintain your form,
even through all the waves intense.
So you must search for Saturn each day,
entirely devoted on your path ahead,
questing valiantly without delay,
transcending each peril as you tread."

So with purpose I did prepare
my sturdy ship, ready to traverse,
reaching the welcoming port near,
sensing then the revitalizing air,
in my mission to completely immerse,
beginning my journey without fear,
and I set out on those seas vast,
ready through various islands to steer,
resolute with my towering mast,
on my crucial search for Saturn dear.

The Former Climber

A curious man I once found,
who as a tranquil star did beam,
radiating with serenity as he did abound,
while all the agitating winds did seem
to stop when he came around,
his appearance perhaps a dream.
I was compelled to quickly question
this intriguing man's ways,
to understand his unique perception,
and he replied without delays.

"I once climbed mountains in this land,
eager to reach each formidable peak,
each majestic achievement grand,
always striving as I continually did seek
the joy of accomplishment, to stand
proudly upon the summit, that crown
of glorious recognition to attain,
always questing further and for more,
widely known through many a town
through all that struggle and strain,
with my tireless efforts to soar,
as I continued relentlessly to train.

Yet when I reached a pinnacle high,
the joy was insufficient and short,
with no deep satisfaction to last,
even with all that arduous labour to fly,
the pleasure collapsing as a fallen fort,
a sinking vessel with a severed mast,
as a dire emptiness would ensue,
that infuriating enemy which did attack,
and that tedious ennui which grew,

always besieged by that anguishing lack.
So I would climb another mountain tall,
aching for that drop of joy ahead,
expending so much energy in the pursuit,
never intending my mission to stall
even through the difficult pain to tread,
determined to find that fleeting fruit.
But again when the peak I did reach,
swiftly the minute joy would disappear,
and once more the emptiness would arrive,
that immense chasm which did breach
my hopes and views, which I held dear,
with never any fulfillment to derive.

So after many summits I finally did halt
my cherished endeavor, that mission vain,
which I once so ardently did exalt,
realizing its futility, and this human state,
which in its disappointment did only drain
my weary mind, chasing pleasures which fade,
so speedily to dissatisfy and wane,
while we are burdened by the weight
of all the vast suffering which does raid.
Now those mountains I no longer scale,
as I've conquered all my old yearnings prior,
tired of life's grueling grief as we wail,
as I search now for freedom from the fire."

The Old Sailor

He had been searching for years
through the tempestuous seas alone,
questing for a certain island of renown,
battling the harsh wind and all his fears,
enduring the storms with his every groan,
so distant now from his childhood town.
From his perilous home he had fled,
with all its constant war and pain,
disillusioned by the struggling toil,
the recurring sorrow to always dread.
Dissatisfied with life which did drain,
he had heard of an abundant island far,
eager to depart from his native soil,
as he left behind every old scar,
towards this new serenity to attain,
seeking this joyful island of peace,
free of distress and every stain,
not willing his strong efforts to cease.

Filled with his ardently fierce fire,
his surging longing was intense,
consumed by this overpowering desire,
as vast as the difficult seas immense.
And so he continued on his path
through the lonely waves dark,
further into the remote waters cold,
hunting with his disappointed wrath,
aspiring to maintain his hopeful spark
and that initial ambition bold.
Yet with an increasingly weary mind,
with the torment of this long quest,
still this island he was unable to find,
yearning so deeply for tranquil rest.

And the old sailor then did meet
with another vessel on its way,
the first encounter of this kind,
now eager the other captain to greet,
rejuvenated to converse on this day,
as their ships were now aligned;
his mission he did promptly explain,
and all the woes he did endure,
not able all his agitation to contain,
as the cruel winds continued to stir,
always battling the unrelenting sky,
speaking of that elusive island obscure,
as he received now a concerned reply
from his counterpart who did assure.

"I too have suffered and wandered long,
with similar aspirations as I did yearn,
my voracious appetite always strong,
until finally I did realize and learn.
I now come to these waters to assist
those like you who still in agony ache,
trapped in the stormy and miserable mist,
as I must urge you now to forsake.
That which you so desperately seek
is really not out there to be found,
but the glorious mountain's peak,
the bliss which always does resound,
is actually inside and deep in your core,
as you must strive now to know
not some distant island's shore,
but your true self, its nature pristine,
that fountain of joy continually to flow,
truly always boundless and serene."

The Visitor

In those wondrous older days,
there was a certain sage of might,
who so loved all of humanity high,
always compassionate in his ways,
seeing himself reflected in their light,
turning to sick children as they would cry;
yet when this adored sage older grew,
in his draining fatigue, increasingly weak,
he finally to a remote cave withdrew,
turning to contemplation as he did seek
the necessary tranquility while he knew
that his body not much longer would last,
not willing as often to openly speak,
his remaining days on the earth few.
And yet even with that distance vast
between his cave and the nearest town,
many the long path were willing to brave,
making that persistent pilgrimage to meet
this knowledgeable elder of renown,
as his assistance they keenly did crave,
approaching him with their tired feet,
and so eager all his wisdom to greet.

But as more visitors continued to arrive,
he was flooded by disappointment immense
for humanity, with all their voracious desire,
always looking to transiently thrive,
as only basic minds he still did sense,
not able to tame their ravenous fire,
with their precious lives swiftly to squander,
worried that the majority only did wander.
Suddenly a new visitor did appear,

his turn to enter the sage's space,
now walking closer with reverence dear
with much seriousness on his face.

"Welcome my friend. And how can I assist?
Are you like the many, like all the rest,
only searching for wealth, never to resist,
searching for more power and on a quest
for love and every earthly pleasure,
always attached to your fleeting nest,
so hungry for that fame beyond measure,
a covetous child then like my every guest?"

And replying firmly to the sage grand
was this weary visitor, with his will strong.
"No, I've suffered too much in this land.
It is only the Truth for which I long."

To Soar

My precious wings I must heal
to finally soar past this prison of pain,
to be free of this anguished wheel,
as these perplexing days I sustain
in this restless sea, always forlorn,
where I must cleanse my sight to know
that cherished refuge to which I turn,
charting ahead with my sails torn
towards the serene waters which flow,
continuing this aching cold to bear,
as for that embracing harbour I yearn,
always to strive for that purest air.

The Knight and the Monk

A weary knight, wounded and forlorn,
in the distance a monastery saw,
deciding finally to stop and rest,
as existence he now did scorn,
no longer viewing the world with awe,
but as a cruel and useless test.
Welcomed kindly, he now did explain
to the sympathetic monk inside
his situation on the lowly plain,
and all his sorrow which did collide
with his once optimistic sense,
as into some dire abyss he did slide,
with tears as he did commence,
eager all his struggles to confide.

"Recently I had this dream
of this glorious lady to behold,
who with such wonder did beam,
who seemed of a celestial mold,
who in every way was ideal,
with her brilliant, inspired mind,
perfect with her stunning face,
as her gaze so swiftly did bind,
leaving me dazed as I did reel,
while she seemed in a remote land,
her vague home difficult to trace,
as she captivated with her appeal,
and after this dream did unwind,
I quickly set out with new zeal
to search for this lady grand,
yearning so intensely to embrace,
desperate this beauty to find,
venturing widely with ardent pace.

Stirred onward by her eyes sublime,
I've voyaged on foreign land and sea,
searching for a substantial time,
first facing vicious pirates who did raid,
close to death until I finally did flee,
then traveling through forests dense,
enduring the cold which did pervade
through the arduous winter intense,
worried some days that I would fade,
as I weakened in energy and health,
bearing many solitary nights dark
and passing enemy kingdoms in stealth,
fighting marauding robbers which mark
the grueling path towards the unknown,
on my lonely trek which did exhaust,
while I have yet to find her, still alone
and deteriorating as insignificant dust
with my suffocating agony in the frost,
disdaining this life now as I must,
not worth its painful cost."

"I'm sorry my friend to hear
of all the anguish you do bear,
but I hope now that I can steer
you ahead towards the serene air.
Human love can indeed provide
great elation and emotional height,
through the years as you stride
together in that jubilant delight,
yet ultimately this joy, as I must say,
is transient and insufficient in its way.
Really that joy for which you seek,
which compels your long pursuit far,

this journey which has made you weak,
burdened by every ache and scar,
that joy truly can be found deep,
deep in your pure, perennial star,
a boundless bliss, lasting and complete,
your nature itself, always to keep,
beyond all the limitations which bar,
greater than any human love can meet.
So with great care I must now advise
that you renounce this chase vain,
away from all the suffering you spurn,
away from every lacking, fleeting prize;
you need freedom from the chain,
and to your true home you must return."

'This is the world of pain'

This is the world of pain,
of samsara and deep anguish,
never to be satisfied on this plane,
wandering again as we languish,
while our bodies weaken and decay
with our recurring agony and toil,
as the mind torments in its way,
as we're still tilling this barren soil.
Each a bundle of unfulfilled desires,
our aching aspirations never cease,
immersed in these ravaging fires,
trapped in this bondage to deplore,
in this struggle without any peace,
with these battles raging in our core.
We continue to labour in our sweat,
yet the disappointment is always clear,
the gap between reality and the ideal,
as countless dreams remain unmet,
continuing through tempests to steer
with all our persistence and zeal,
yet the inevitable suffering deep
always arrives as we only weep.

Yet the world of the Absolute to adore
is free of all this pain and sorrow,
full of endless bliss evermore,
the wondrous hope of tomorrow,
a boundless ocean, clear and pure,
with joyful consciousness complete,
with never any distress to stir,
our true home, as we await our seat
in union with the infinite and serene,
yearning with that glory to meet,

to know our true nature pristine,
with that sublime wonder to greet.
Yet the immense difficulty now lies
in the solitary pathway to transcend,
to soar beyond every earthly scourge,
the excruciating cycle to finally end.
Deeply longing to see and rise,
this mighty struggle does emerge,
this pursuit beyond even the mind,
the quest the Absolute to finally find.

The Lion and the Eagle

"As the pervasive pain is dire,
I'm deeply dissatisfied with this life,
with this endless unfulfilled desire,
these desires which only multiply,
trapped here in this desert of strife,
as only nothingness does underlie,
as these empty days only tire,
still chained and never able to fly,
always aching in this agonizing fire,
and bewildered as I turn to the sky."

And so the sage, who he did revere,
replied with his vital message dear.
"On your path, this is a crucial day,
as life's deep suffering you recognize,
seeing with clarity that you are bound,
as this pain now pushes you in its way,
as you yearn for liberation, to rise,
as now the Infinite must be found.

Yet faith and belief are not enough,
as you cross this tempestuous sea,
while these recurring winds are rough,
as only with great effort will you be free.
The only way now to truly end
all the suffering which you endure
is to strive with focus to transcend,
to find your true essence pure,
as against the lion you must defend,
even as it relentlessly does stir,
that beast which always does attack,
returning again, voracious on this plain,

which leaves you with that sense of lack,
the source of such vicious pain.
But working to ascend, you must aspire
to quiet the ruthless lion's roar,
that cruel creature finally to expire,
as the eagle must triumph and soar,
as you must remove the stubborn veil,
with that deeper knowledge to gain,
with continued fortitude as you sail,
voyaging back home as you maintain
your path through each testing gale,
with that serenity to soon attain.

Identify not with the lion, the proud king,
in restless anguish for greater power,
always in hunger, searching for more,
but turn instead to the sacred wing,
to the eagle which is meant to tower,
that underlying bliss at your very core.
And as you move beyond all the mist,
eventually you shall come to understand
that the lion doesn't even really exist,
but only the pristine and majestic eagle grand,
with its triumphant light continually to beam,
united with the one Consciousness Supreme."

The Seer of the Island

I was immersed in this battle fierce,
trapped in this raging naval clash
in the chaos of the turbulent sea,
as the waves did violently smash,
while my worries continued to pierce,
longing through all my anguish to flee
that struggle which seemed without end,
as that formidable enemy of might
continued always mercilessly to send
more powerful ships into the fight,
with many injured comrades to treat
and those fires engulfing each fleet.

Finally a tempest pulled me away,
throwing me suddenly to a distant shore,
no longer under combat's vicious sway,
as I was deeply grateful then to land,
finding some relief in my battered core,
as I walked ahead, curiously in my way,
exploring the small island, as I found
this humble dwelling which did stand,
approaching while the wind did pound,
and hoping for a friendly sound.

I was welcomed by the inhabitant old,
who then graciously led me inside,
and soon his address he did mold,
eager that night to share and confide.
"I am a disciple of Pythagoras sublime,
who continued the Orphic wisdom high;
I am a disciple too of Empedocles dear,
of Parmenides of that glorious time,

of cherished Plato who shall always fly,
and of Plotinus who we must revere.
Follow me and the way I will show
to be free of all the pain you endure,
guided by my maps as you will know
the blissful waters, pristine and pure."

And in the glorious morning I did feel
completely renewed and without fear,
as my anguished wounds did heal,
and all the winds did disappear,
as I was absorbed in calmness serene,
with a jubilant bird swiftly soaring past,
over that wondrous island green
which always in my memory shall last,
as that cosmic harmony I then did hear,
embraced by those sunbeams clear.

Pain and Sorrow

I'm always plagued by this deep pain,
endless as the forsaken wilderness vast,
this empty desolation which does chain,
as a damaged vessel with its mast
plunging down into the depths dark,
leaving me only in this agony to drown,
while this vile sorrow does destroy
as a besieging enemy without end,
as countless invading armies they deploy,
my crumbling walls swiftly coming down,
as this cruel burden continues to mark
all my days, no longer that jubilant boy
who looked with such wonder at the world,
fated from that cherished time to descend
into this miserable void, as I was hurled
bewilderingly into this futile, wretched land
with all my wounds impossible to mend,
forced to carry this excruciating weight,
questioning the universe as I withstand
the constant anguish of my state.
And when the day's work is complete,
and I finally attempt to find some rest,
longing for a quiet, peaceful seat,
the pain resurfaces again from my core,
more severe in that lonely, evening hour,
the relentless void returning to test,
while I'm weary and lacking power,
always forced to resume this war.

On Joy

Everyone is searching for joy,
always chasing that jubilation grand,
from the business man to the playing boy,
striving with so much effort to rejoice,
as that common longing is heard
continuously in this difficult land
by each aspiring, individual voice,
which envies the freedom of the bird,
and even through our struggles long,
joy in many forms can be found,
with momentary harmony in life's song,
beaming radiantly as it does resound.
And yet the mature soul will realize
that this joy is really never enough,
as only tiny drops in a sea of pain,
never fulfilled by each passing prize,
always fleeting through the winds rough,
while this existence continues to chain,
and then that soul will turn their eyes
finally inward to begin the crucial quest
towards that which has always been there,
beyond the limited and finite to rise,
towards that which everything did manifest,
and beyond even the greatest skies,
past all human suffering and despair,
no longer in aching distress to roam,
finally with pure consciousness aware
of the infinite joy which is our home.

The Captain

The captain reached the shore
of an abundant island of fruit,
with the welcoming land to adore,
as the coveted rest now did suit
his tired mind and suffering core,
as he conversed with an elder astute,
the local listening with intrigued eyes
to the veteran captain as he did relate
the details of his long voyage to prize,
and the all anguish of his current state.

"My wondrous childhood I recall,
back in the joy of my cherished home,
when such serenity pervaded all,
and those pure fields I would roam.
Yet I experienced that growing desire
for independence, the need to explore,
that urge to separate which did emerge,
my fierce compulsion as a raging fire,
always searching, longing for more,
as my soaring aspirations did surge.
As my passion for the waves grew,
I labored fervently to prepare,
finally obtaining my ship to depart,
and gathering my devoted crew,
my officers who always support,
ready for the open ocean's air,
strategizing my bold path to chart,
as I headed to my country's port,
through the waters as I did tear,
and ready for any dangers to court.
Leaving the comfort of my native land,
with such vibrant energy I did sail,

questing with my ambitions grand,
and fearlessly confronting each gale,
as I was so eager to achieve,
making those discoveries great,
with many distant islands to perceive,
so many new lands which did await.

Yet after all I did gratefully attain,
this ruthless weariness I now sense,
battered by this plaguing pain,
left in this dreary abyss of dismay,
this abyss which is truly immense,
as the mist obscures my view,
this fog which is always a bane,
immersed in this bewildering grey,
in this agitation as I continue to stew,
and I yearn so deeply for the day
when I will return to my precious plain,
back to my beloved home true."

The elder promptly did reply,
understanding the captain's distress,
aligned with the harmony of the sky,
as his visitor he now did address.
"The path home is difficult and long,
and many actually do not arrive,
not yet ready, nor sufficiently strong,
as they prefer instead to thrive
in the easier ways they apprehend,
as it takes a great man to derive
the courage and focus deep
to concentrate entirely and mend
their ways, no longer then to weep,
to finally fill that aching inner hole,
purifying their inner waters to reap

the fulfillment of that glorious goal.
Yet you have reached a crucial part
of your travels, a momentous stage,
as those growing waters flow,
as you are aware now of the cage,
with the rising need in your heart
for your home once again to know.
As into your valiant eyes I now gaze,
I believe that you have the strength
to free yourself of this painful haze,
truly ready for that voyage of length."

Grateful for his words wise,
the inspired captain now did leave
that plentiful island, that safe rest,
as he prepared ardently to rise
beyond his mind which did grieve,
beyond all the agony which did test.
Soon the weather did quickly turn,
as the darkening sky did appall,
those recurring gales always to spurn,
as to his crewmen he now did call,
readying them for the cruel churn,
which their course would surely stall.
And he encountered the vicious storm,
with relentless winds which did attack,
the tempest surpassing the norm,
as he thought often of turning back,
filled again with swelling doubt,
as the waves were increasingly fierce,
worried that the vessel wouldn't hold,
that the sea would eventually pierce,
the crew panicking with each shout,
as the desperate chaos did enfold.
Anticipating the possible breach,

he struggled under the stress to endure,
his destination seeming so remote to reach,
as those furious winds continued to stir.

And yet finally the storm did subside,
appreciative now of the calmer air,
amazed that the vessel did withstand,
as the luminous stars did graciously guide
his resolute path, as he did share
much joy with his crew, closely allied,
as their devoted energies did expand,
after all that mayhem they did bear.
So onward the captain did proceed,
as there was still much distance ahead,
still necessary many waves to traverse,
yet he felt now the emerging seed
of new glory in which to immerse,
through this arduous mission to tread.
He was determined to carry through,
while expecting more storms to face,
those hazards which would likely ensue,
ready with all his fortitude to brace.

The captain nourished his hope of might
that eventually he would truly see
his native port, with his home to unite,
to embrace again his childhood tree.
With persistent trust as he did yearn,
he sought the radiance of his city's beam,
assured that he would soon return
to that pure bliss, to always teem.

The Soul's Voyage

The individual soul, continuing to grow
over many lifetimes on its arduous course,
ultimately longs and strives to know
the glory of the Absolute, the Ultimate Source,
that which pervades and underpins all,
manifesting this harmonious cosmos grand,
which it does boundlessly transcend,
the principle on which everything does stand,
which by numerous names many call,
which through each person does beam,
as we progress valiantly to this highest end,
to the Infinite and Eternal Supreme,
for freedom from all limitation and pain,
which must inevitably become our aim,
triumphant over all suffering and fear,
questing to soar beyond the relative plane,
beyond the veil which does appear,
to realize then our essence to be the same
as the one Absolute and always unified,
while the illusory must fade as mist,
as we yearn so blissfully to be tied
with that which shall always exist;
and through all of our struggle we gain,
voyaging with our endless might,
towards beaming knowledge to attain,
with the Godhead to finally unite.

.

Made in the USA
Middletown, DE
25 April 2019